SHERLOCK BONES LOOKS AT
PHYSICAL SCIENCE

Electricity

Harriet McGregor

WINDMILL
BOOKS
New York

3 1257 02365 7298

Published in 2011 by Windmill Books, LLC
303 Park Avenue South, Suite #1280, New York, NY 10010-3657

First Edition

Senior Editor: Camilla Lloyd
Designer: Simon Borrough
Consultant: Jon Turney
Picture Researcher: Amy Sparks
Illustrator: Stefan Chabluk
Sherlock Bones Artwork: Richard Hook

Photographs:
Abbreviations: t-top, b-bottom, l-left, r-right, m-middle.
Cover: Shutterstock (3imediaphoto); **Insides: Folios** Shutterstock (Jim Barber):
1 Dreamstime (Bosenok); 4 Dreamstime (tl Jocic, tlc Paul George Bodea, trc Adrian
Coroama, tr Charles Brutlag, bl Mike Tan, br Kingjon); 5 Corbis (Darryl Bush/San
Francisco); 6 Dreamstime (Mangia); 7 Dreamstime (Bright); 9 Corbis (The Art Archive);
10 Getty (Greg Ceo); 13 Corbis (Andrew Lichtenstein); 15 Dreamstime (Bosenok);
16 Dreamstime (tr Nexus7, bl Gsermek, bc Vtorous, br Josefbosak); 17 Shutterstock
(Jim Barber); 19 Dreamstime (Witr); 20 (l) Istockphoto (John Blair), 20 (r) Dreamstime
(Cammeraydave); 21 Dreamstime (Edward Bock); 22 Alamy (isifa Image Service s.r.o.);
23 Photolibrary; 26 Shutterstock (3imediaphoto); 27 Photolibrary.

Library of Congress Cataloging-in-Publication Data

McGregor, Harriet.
 Electricity / by Harriet McGregor. — 1st ed.
    p. cm. — (Sherlock Bones looks at physical science)
 Includes index.
 ISBN 978-1-61533-210-6 (library binding)
 1. Electricity—Juvenile literature. I. Title.
 QC527.2.M42 2011
 537—dc22
                                    2010024562

Manufactured in China

For more great fiction and nonfiction, go to www.windmillbooks.com

CPSIA Compliance Information: Batch #WAW1102W: For Further Information contact Windmill Books, New York, New York on 1-866-478-0556

Contents

Words that appear in **bold** can be found in the glossary on page 30.

The Science Detective, Sherlock Bones, will help you learn all about Electricity. The answers to Sherlock's questions can be found on page 31.

What Is Electricity?

We use electricity in countless ways every day. An electric alarm clock might wake us up in the morning, we switch on an electric light and go to the bathroom. We might use an electric toothbrush and then make breakfast using a toaster. Electricity can keep our homes warm and our showers hot. Electricity is even needed to start cars, and to power computers, telephones, and televisions.

▲ These devices all need electrical energy to make them work.

THE SCIENCE DETECTIVE INVESTIGATES:

Using Electricity

You will need:
• *notebook* • *pen*

Investigate how many times you use electricity in one day. As you go through your day, pay close attention to what you are doing. Make notes each time you use electricity. Write down the time, the type of electrical device, and the purpose of the device. At the end of the day, count the number of times you used electricity. You might be surprised.

Energy

Electricity is a type of **energy**. Energy is the ability to do **work**. Humans get energy from food and **oxygen**. Food is digested inside our bodies and gives us energy to move, think, speak, and grow.

Electrical energy makes bulbs light, washing machines spin, and heaters give out heat. In each of these devices, electrical energy is turned into another type of energy. Light bulbs give out light energy, washing machines turn electrical energy into movement energy, and heaters produce heat energy.

STAY SAFE

Although electricity can be very dangerous, there are ways to keep safe.

- Never use electrical devices near sources of water, such as the bathtub, sink, or shower.
- Never touch electrical devices with wet hands.
- Never play with electrical plugs, switches, and cables.
- Stay away from overhead power lines and pylons.
- Do not play outside during a thunderstorm.
- Watch for the symbols that warn you of the dangers of electricity.
- Stay away from electrified railroad tracks.

There are lots of types of energy. Can you think of five? See if you can take this total to ten by doing an Internet search.

▼ The games console and the user need energy to play the game. The game needs electrical energy and the user needs energy from food.

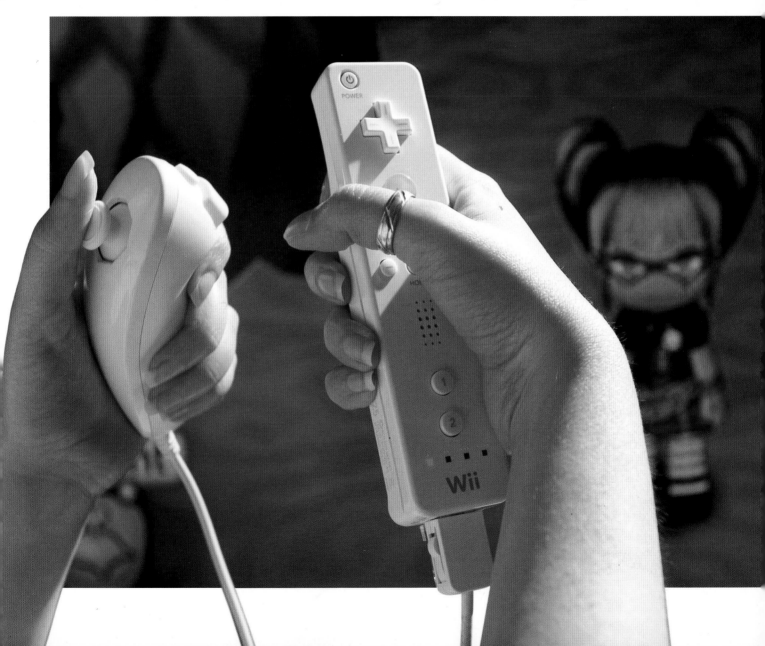

Where Does Electricity Come From?

All electrical devices get their energy to work from either **household electricity** or **batteries**. Televisions and microwaves plug into a wall socket. They use household electricity. The electricity travels from the wall socket, down the cable, and into the device. Electrical energy makes the device work.

Electricity's Journey

Most household electricity comes from huge factories called **power stations**. In a power station, a **fuel** is burned. The fuel is often natural gas or coal. The burning fuel heats water. Steam from the water turns large fans called **turbines**. The turbines spin a **generator**, which makes electricity. In power stations, the energy in fuel is turned into electrical energy. **Alternative energy**, such as wind and solar energy, can also be made into electricity (see page 27).

SCIENCE AT WORK

Not all electricity comes from power stations and batteries. Lightning is a type of electricity called **static electricity**. It is produced in clouds during thunderstorms. When enough static electricity builds up in clouds, it jumps either to the ground or to another cloud. We see the bolt of lightning and hear a bang of thunder. The thunder is caused by the lightning heating the air very suddenly.

▲ Lightning has a temperature of around 50,000°F (28,000°C), which is approximately five times hotter than the surface of the Sun.

Electricity travels to homes and schools along heavy cables. The cables run underground in cities, but overground in open areas. Large pylons hold the cables high above ground. Pylons are very tall, metal towers.

The electricity carried by overhead cables is extremely powerful. It is important that pylons hold the cables high above ground because anyone touching the cable could be killed by an **electric shock**.

▲ **Electricity is carried overground and underground in thick, heavy cables in this residential area.**

Why Do We Need Batteries?

Batteries are useful **power sources** because they are portable (easy to carry around) and come in all shapes and sizes. Watches, calculators, and hearing aids use tiny button batteries. Flashlights use different-sized batteries, depending on the size of the flashlight.

Energy from Batteries

Batteries are stores of energy. They contain chemicals. Each battery has a positive and a negative terminal. Electricity is produced when a wire is connected to the positive and negative terminals of the battery. The electricity flows from the negative terminal, through the wire, and back to the positive terminal.

THE SCIENCE DETECTIVE INVESTIGATES:

Match the Battery

Look carefully at the batteries shown in the pictures. Which battery is found in which of the following devices?

Remote control

Cell phone

Watch

Car

1

2

3

4

Battery Life

A battery's energy store does not last forever. Battery life depends on the device that it powers. Some devices need more electricity than others. These devices make a battery run down quickly.

Cell phones and some cameras use small batteries that can be **recharged** by plugging them into an electric socket for a short time. This means that they can be used again and again. Some windup radios and flashlights contain rechargeable batteries. When they are wound up, the battery is recharged.

The types of battery in small flashlights are safe to use in investigations. Button batteries and car batteries are not safe to use. You should never take apart any type of battery.

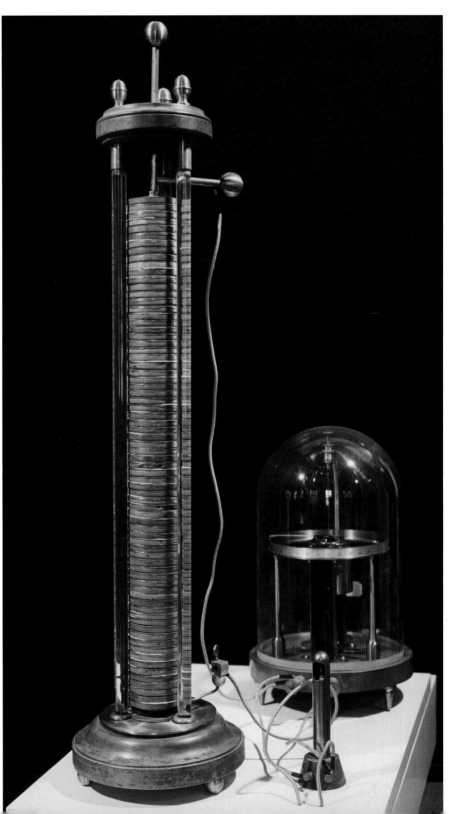

▼ The voltaic pile was the first battery to produce a continuous supply of electricity.

SCIENCE AT WORK

Alessandro Volta invented the first battery in 1799. It was called the voltaic pile. It was made of piles of copper and zinc disks, separated by pieces of flannel soaked in a chemical solution.

Why Do We Use Circuits?

Circuits let us use electricity. They connect the lights in schools, the wall sockets of a house and the electrical systems in a car. They are present in remote controls, computers, traffic lights, refrigerators, and all other electrical devices. Computer **microchips** have tiny circuits. Office buildings contain large circuits. Circuits can even be the size of a whole country.

Series and Parallel Circuits

A **series circuit** is one loop of wire with components connected in it. The electricity travels from the battery, along the wire, and through every component before it returns to the battery. Imagine a series circuit that contains one power source and many Christmas tree light bulbs. If any of the light bulbs blow, the circuit will no longer work and none of the bulbs will light. The blown light bulb creates a gap in the circuit and the electricity is stopped from flowing.

▲ A series circuit with one battery and two bulbs.

A **parallel circuit** has more than one loop of wire. In a parallel circuit, the electricity leaves the battery and then splits to travel down more than one loop of wire. Imagine a parallel circuit with two loops of wire. Each loop of wire carries one light bulb. If one of the bulbs blows, electricity can still continue around the other loop and light the bulb.

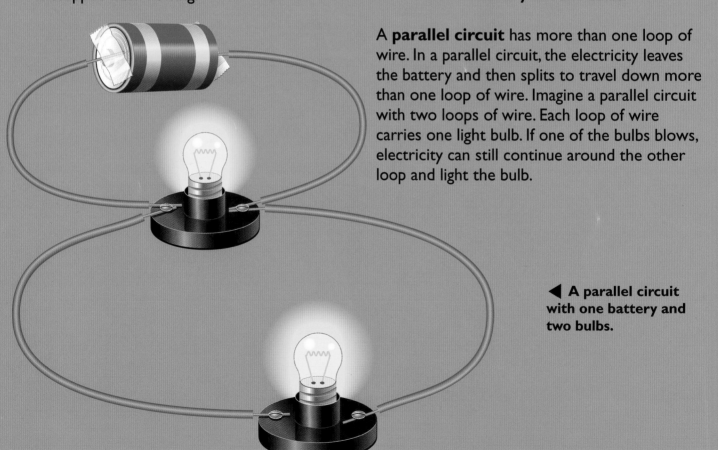

◀ A parallel circuit with one battery and two bulbs.

The National Grid

In the United States, almost every building, streetlight, and traffic signal is connected in a huge circuit. This circuit is called the **national grid**. When electricity leaves power stations, it enters the power cables that make up the national grid. The electricity is very powerful and has a high **voltage**. As it travels through the power cables, its voltage is changed. By the time it reaches your house, the voltage is much lower, although it is still powerful enough to be very dangerous.

▲ Skyscraper lights are connected in parallel. At night, the lights on a whole floor can be turned off, while the lights on other floors can stay lit.

How Can You Change a Circuit?

Circuits can have extra components added to them or components can be taken away. The effect on the circuit depends on what is changed.

▼ Radio controlled cars contain a motor and a battery pack. The battery pack provides just the right amount of power for the motor.

▲ The electric eel lives on the muddy bottoms of rivers in South America. It can give an electrical shock of up to 500 volts.

SCIENCE AT WORK

Electric fish can make electricity. They use it to stun their prey, navigate their way through the water, communicate with other fish, or detect objects in the water. Usually, an electric organ in the tail of the fish makes the electricity. The bolts of electricity can give a nasty shock.

Brighter and Faster

When extra batteries are added to a circuit, the device works harder—the motor runs more quickly or the bulb glows more brightly. Be careful not to add too many batteries. Bulbs and motors are designed to be used with batteries of a certain voltage. If the voltage of the batteries is too great, the device may burn out. For example, a 1.5 volt bulb needs a 1.5 volt battery. Taking away batteries makes a motor run more slowly or makes a bulb glow less brightly.

Extra Bulbs

As more bulbs are added to a circuit, they glow less brightly. In a circuit with one battery, two bulbs will glow less brightly than one bulb. The two bulbs will glow with the same level of brightness—one will not glow more brightly than the other.

Types of Wire

Electricity finds it easier to travel through thick wire than through very thin wire. A thin wire provides more **resistance** to the flow of electricity. A bulb will glow less brightly in a circuit that contains very thin wire. It will glow more brightly in a circuit that contains thick wire. Lengthening the wire in a circuit can also make a bulb glow less brightly.

Your Project: How Does the Thickness of Wire Change a Bulb's Brightness?

I f a very thin wire is connected in a circuit, what effect will this have on a light bulb? First, make a prediction about what you think might happen. In this case, the prediction could be: *Thin wire added to a circuit will change the brightness of the bulb.* Use the information below to conduct your own investigation.

Hypothesis

A hypothesis is a statement about what you think might happen in your investigation. For this experiment, it could be: *In a circuit with one battery and one bulb, a thin wire added to the circuit causes the bulb to glow less brightly.*

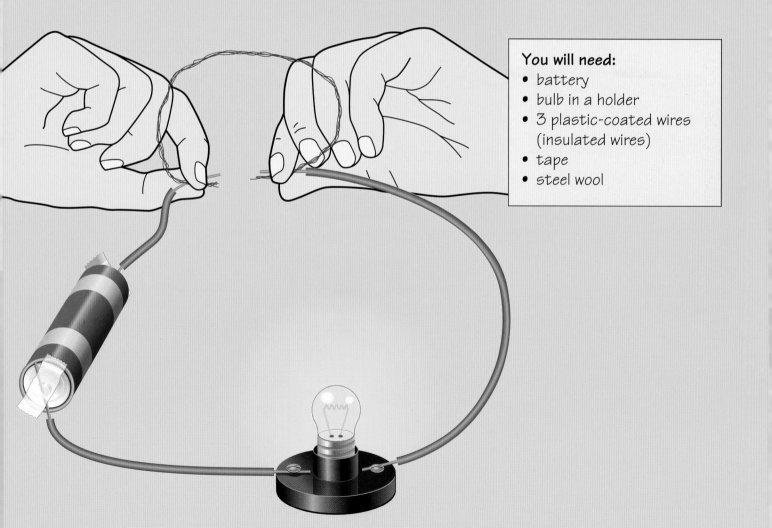

You will need:
- battery
- bulb in a holder
- 3 plastic-coated wires (insulated wires)
- tape
- steel wool

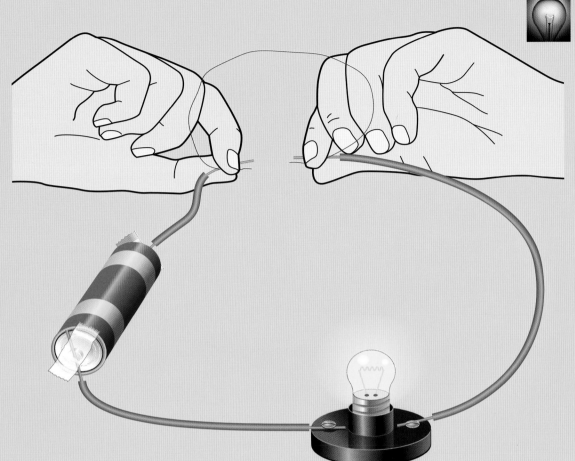

Method

1 Use tape to connect one wire to the positive terminal of the battery and another wire to the negative terminal of the battery.
2 Connect the bulb to one of the battery wires. Attach the third wire to the other side of the bulb.
3 Unravel some of the steel wool to make a strand of wire. It should be roughly as thick as your insulated wires.
4 Hold the wire that you have made so that it is touching the two loose ends of the insulated wires to complete the circuit.
5 Look at the bulb. Is it glowing?
6 Make the steel wool thinner by removing some of the strands.
7 Connect it back into the circuit and look at the bulb. Is it brighter or dimmer?
8 Make the steel wool even thinner and connect it into the circuit again. Is the bulb brighter or dimmer?

🐾 A fair test is one in which only one part of an investigation is changed at a time. Is your method a fair test? If it is, how do you know this? What is your conclusion?

What Happened and Why?

Your results should show that as the steel wool strand is made thinner and thinner, the light bulb glows less brightly. Electricity finds it hard to travel through thin wires. They provide resistance. When the wire is very thin, only a small electrical current (a small amount of electricity) travels around the circuit. The bulb cannot glow brightly with such a small electrical current.

Index